# Getting started

Hi

You may have never really read the Bible before, but we are s

God says that He wants to talk to us from His Word (the Bible

Try to read a section each day – it will only take a few minute:

where you won't be disturbed or distracted.

Each day,

**1** *Pray a short prayer, asking God to help you understand the text you are going to read.*

**2** *Read the Bible passage, then the page from your notes.*

**3** *Think about what you have read.*

**4** *Have a go at answering the questions.*

**5** *In a short prayer, ask God to help you put into practice what you have learnt from the story. If you have learnt something about God or Jesus, praise and thank Him. Spend a short time praying about people you know, and your day ahead.*

**6** *Don't be tempted to rush ahead on to the next day!*

Have you ever warned someone of something that was going to happen? Perhaps a surprise, so that the person can prepare beforehand and get ready by tidying the house for a visitor, or buying a new outfit for a special event. In our reading today, we read that John the Baptist did just that for the Jewish people. He warned them that God's Deliverer was coming soon and they needed to get ready. John wore strange clothes and ate strange food.

**?** *What did he wear? (v6)*

clothing of camel

**?** *What did he eat? (v6)*

locusts + wild honey

We need to get ready to hear what God has to say to us through this book of Mark.

Mark 1:9–13

In these verses, we read that Jesus was baptised. This was to show that He agreed with the message that John was preaching.

**? How do you know that God was pleased with Jesus? (v11)**

........................................................

Even Jesus was tempted to do wrong, but because He was perfect, He never gave in to temptation. When you are tempted to do wrong, always remember to pray – Jesus understands because He's been there!

# Following Jesus

After John the Baptist was put in prison, Jesus started to preach.

**? What did He preach? (v15)**

..................................................................

You may think that you are a very ordinary person, and yet, Jesus chose very ordinary people to follow Him (v17). Simon and Andrew did not hesitate to follow Jesus when He called them.

**? Do you hesitate to follow Jesus?**

..................................................................

**? What was Simon and Andrew's job? (v16)**

..................................................................

72 days with Mark

## No match for Jesus

Have you ever been to church and thought that the preacher was boring? You wouldn't have thought like that if you had been there when Jesus was preaching! People listened to Him and realised that He was very special. Even Satan's followers, the demons, knew that Jesus was special and that they were no match for Him. He spoke, and they obeyed. They had no choice! (v26) How powerful Jesus is! As Jesus freed this poor man, who had been controlled by demons, He showed how kind and caring He was.

**Who did the evil spirit say Jesus was? (v24)**

.......................................................................................

Mark 1:29–39

70 days with Mark

Have you ever had a new toy and it seemed like everyone wanted to be your friend so that they could play with it? Or, have you ever had a big bag of sweets that suddenly made you become very popular? This was what Jesus may have felt like in today's reading. Everywhere He went people wanted to crowd around Him because He had the power to heal. Eventually He had to move on, as He wanted to tell others the Good News.

**?** *What was more important – to hear the 'Good News' or to see miracles? (v38)*

........................................................

**?** *What did the lady do after Jesus had healed her? (v31)*

........................................................

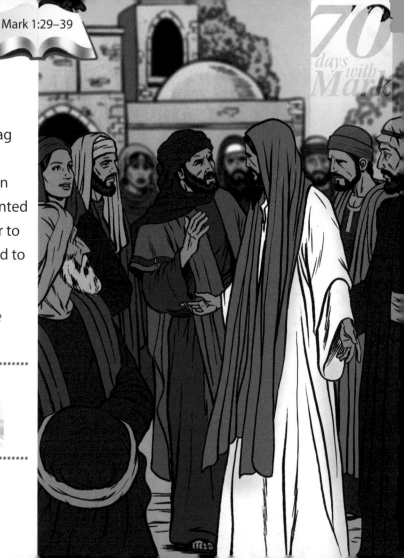

Mark 1:40–45

How wonderful Jesus is! He cared for those who no one else would go near. Here we read of a man with a nasty skin disease. No one would want to get near him never mind touch him. But Jesus loved him and cared enough to touch the man and heal him. No wonder the man wanted to tell everyone! Are you excited about telling other people about Jesus?

**?**

*How long did it take Jesus to heal the man with the skin disease? (v42)*

.......................................................

Have you got any friends who need the help of Jesus? Pray for them. Jesus cares for people very much. Here we see that Jesus has tremendous power, not only to heal, but also to forgive people's sins. Which of these two do you think is the most important? No ordinary man can heal or forgive, but Jesus isn't an ordinary man is He?

**?** *Jesus has just forgiven a man his sins. Who does that mean Jesus really is? ( See v7)*

**?** *What was wrong with the man in this story? (v3)*

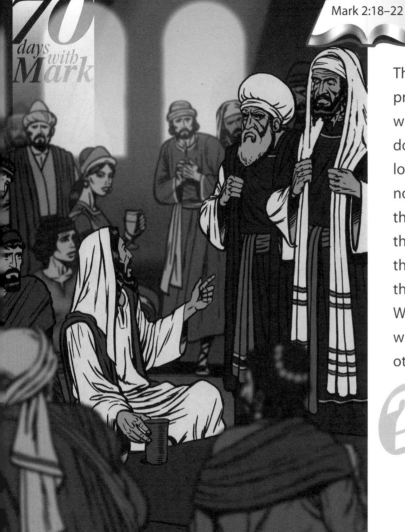

# Show off!

There is nothing worse than a 'show off' – a person pretending to be better than they really are. This is what the religious people (Pharisees) were doing. They had given up eating to make themselves look good, and criticised the followers of Jesus for not doing the same. Jesus explains that they should think about why they behave like this, and tells them they need to change their hearts. He goes on to say that He won't be with them much longer. After this there will be time for sadness and giving up eating. When we do things for God, we need to think about why we are doing them.  Is it for God, or to impress others?

*Who did Jesus say He was like? (v19–20)*

..............................................................

**Rules, rules, rules**

Mark 2:23–28

The religious leaders who we read about yesterday had not learnt their lesson after Jesus had spoken to them. Was it because they hadn't understood or just that they didn't want to listen? Again, they criticise the followers of Jesus for not keeping rules. The 'Sabbath' was Saturday, a day the Jews kept holy for God. The religious leaders were more interested in keeping rules than living to please God.

**?** *Which two Old Testament characters did Jesus talk about? (v25–26)*

70 days with Mark

Jesus loved people. Whenever He came across a person with problems, He wanted to help them. Today, we read of a poor man who had a crippled hand. It was useless; he couldn't do anything with it. But, the day he met Jesus in the synagogue, everything changed. Jesus healed him the moment the man reached out to Him (v5). Today, have you got a problem that is worrying you? Why not reach out to Jesus in prayer? He wants to help you.

*After they had seen this wonderful miracle, what did the Pharisees and Herodians plan to do? (v6)*

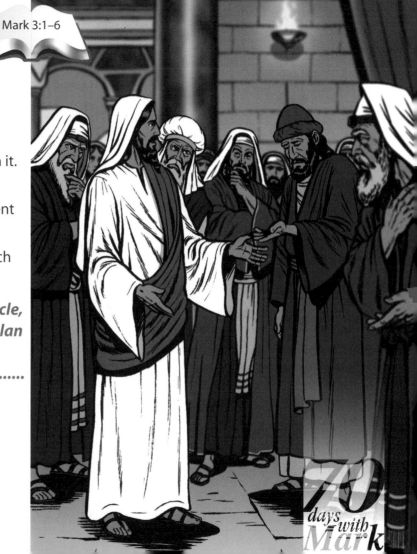

70 days with Mark

Mark 3:7–12

## Wonderful words of Jesus

Here we read of Jesus becoming very popular. Everywhere He goes, crowds gather around Him. Some came to be healed of diseases, some came to be free from the power Satan had over them. Some were there to hear the wonderful words that He spoke.

**?** *What do you think was the most important reason to follow Jesus?*

.........................................................................

**?** *What did Jesus use so that the people wouldn't crowd against Him? (v9)*

.........................................................................

Mark 3:13–19

## Take twelve

Jesus chose twelve men to teach and spend time with, so that they could carry on God's work when He had gone. There was nothing special about these men – they weren't important, rich or famous – just ordinary like you and me. But, they were willing to follow Jesus and obey Him. So Jesus was able to use them greatly. He is able to do the same today with people like us if we are willing to follow and obey Him.

**?** *Can you name three of the men chosen by Jesus?*

...........................................................................................................

Mark 3:20–30

Jesus was performing many miracles.

**?**

*What could Jesus and His followers not do, as the crowds were so large? (v20)*

........................................................

People had never seen anything like it before. The religious leaders were jealous of Jesus because many people started to follow Him instead of them. They accused Jesus of being mad and then receiving the power to do the miracles from Satan. Jesus explained to the people that this was impossible. The miracles He performed were overcoming evil and as Satan is evil, he would be fighting himself. Everything Jesus did was pure and perfect because He is pure and perfect.

70 days with Mark

Mark 3:31–35

Jesus' mother and brothers arrived as they had heard all sorts of rumours about Him and were concerned for Him. When they arrived, Jesus said that all those who trusted Him and followed God were His true family. It is wonderful to know that we, too, can belong to Jesus in such a close way. Are you a member of His family?

**What shows that we belong to God's family? (v35)**

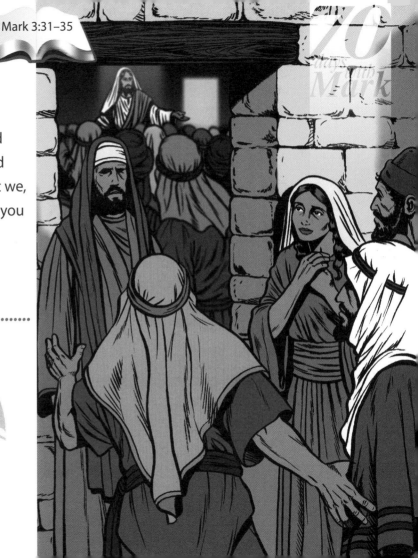

Jesus often used stories to explain very important things to people. He really wanted them to listen and understand His message so they could be saved from their sins. A farmer who was planting seeds was something that everybody knew about in Israel. Jesus used this story to make His point. Do you listen when you read God's Word, the Bible? Jesus longs that you do, and obey it.

**?** *What happened to the seed that fell on the good ground? (v8)*

..................................................................

## Listen, believe and trust

Jesus explains about the story we read yesterday. The seed is like God's Word (the Bible); the soil is like different people's hearts. What is your heart like? Here is a test:

When you hear God's Word explained, or when you read the Bible, do you:

1. Let it go in one ear and out the other. ☐
2. Listen, believe it at first, but soon forget it when friends tease you. ☐
3. Listen and believe but let other things like possessions and hobbies become more important than following God. ☐
4. Listen, believe and trust your whole life to Jesus, and begin to love Him and appreciate Him more and more. ☐

(Tick the one that applies to you.)

70 days with Mark

**DAY 17** Shine for Jesus

Mark 4:21–25

How silly it would be to light a candle and then cover it up! Its main purpose is to shine in the darkness. The message of Good News, which Jesus brought, was the light to shine into the darkness of the world's sin.

**?** *What did Jesus say would happen to all the secret things that take place? (v22)*

.........................................................................

This light had been given to Jesus, and later would be given to those who believed and followed Him. Are you willing to take the message to others and bring light to their lives?

Mark 4:26–29

God's Word, the Bible, is very powerful if people listen to it. It's like a little seed that is planted in the ground and will one day grow to become grain in a field ready to harvest.

**?**

*What happens to the planted seed while the man is sleeping? (v27)*

That is the effect that the Bible can have in people's lives. It will change them and make them grow into God's people. We should always be eager to share God's Word, the precious seed, with others. We just don't know what might happen!

# 70 days with Mark

Mark 4:30–34

## What a change!

Have you ever planted a mustard seed? It is so tiny and yet, if planted in the proper place, will grow very big.

### What did Jesus say happened to the mustard seed? (v32)

..........................................................................

Jesus used this to show what the Good News He was sharing can result in. It might seem very unimportant to some people, but it has far reaching effects. The message has changed so many lives from then and even up to today.

## Facing the storm

What a terrible storm! Even the disciples who were fishermen were afraid, and they were used to the sea. They thought they were going to drown. They had forgotten that Jesus was with them and His great power.

**? Where was Jesus, and what was He doing? (v38)**

.........................................................................

Jesus was able to show His great power over the winds and the waves. In a moment, Jesus changed everything around from panic to calm. If we belong to Jesus we need never be alarmed, whatever is going wrong around us.

70 days with Mark

**DAY 21** A new man!

Mark 5:1–20

The religious leaders never realised who Jesus was – God's promised Messiah. Even the evil spirits (Satan's servants) realised who Jesus was (v7–8). What a difference Jesus made in this man's life. He had been changed from a man who was sad, out of control, and cutting himself with stones (v5–6), to a man who was happy, controlled, and wanting to follow Jesus (v15). How powerful Jesus is!

**?** *After Jesus had changed this man's life, what did the man want to do? (v18)*

..........................................................

**?** *What did Jesus tell him to do? (v19)*

..........................................................

70 days with Mark

# A twelve-year-old problem!

Here we see two people that Jesus healed in a wonderful way. A lady who had been slowly dying for twelve years and a girl that had been living for twelve years.

**?** *What had the sick woman spent all her money on? (v26)*

.......................................................................

Both of them had a problem, which only Jesus could solve. Thankfully, they both met Jesus and He healed them. Who do you go to when you have a problem?

70 days with Mark

# More than a carpenter

Before Jesus had started going around preaching, He had lived a very ordinary life in Nazareth. He had worked as a carpenter, making things out of wood.

**?** *What did Jesus do which caused the people from His hometown to be amazed? (v2)*

Today, we read how He returned there, but very few people believed who He really was – that He was the Son of God. To them, He was just a carpenter, although He was much more than that. This made Jesus very sad and He wasn't able to help them because they didn't want His help.

70 days with Mark

# Head on a plate

When we disobey God there is always a consequence. This often means that others get hurt. Herod had sinned and this led to John the Baptist dying a terrible death.

 **What foolish promise had Herod made to Herodias' daughter? (v22–23)**

................................................................

When you are tempted to do wrong, remember that you may be about to cause much hurt to others.

# The biggest picnic ever!

There is never a problem too big for Jesus. How would you feel about having to provide a picnic for over five thousand people? Well, Jesus did just that with only five loaves and two fish!

**?** *How many baskets were filled with leftovers? (v43)*

•••••••••••••••••••••••••••••••••••••••••••••••••••••••

Time and time again, we see Jesus proving that He was no ordinary man, but truly God.

Mark 6:45–56

The disciples were in big trouble. They were out on the lake and a terrific storm blew up. Even though they were experienced fishermen, the waves were getting the better of them. All the time, Jesus had been watching them (v48) from the shore. He knew the danger they were in and went and saved them.

**?** *Why was Jesus able to walk on the water?*

...........................................................................

**?** *What happened to the storm when Jesus got into the boat? (v51)*

...........................................................................

If we belong to Jesus He watches over us and comes to our help when we need Him.

## Inside or out?

The religious leaders of Jesus' day were more concerned with keeping rules and regulations than listening to Jesus and obeying Him.

***Why were the Pharisees angry with Jesus' disciples? (v5)***

..............................................................

***What is the 5th commandment, which Jesus talks about? (v10)***

..............................................................

They were more concerned with how things looked to other people than how God saw them. If God was to look into your heart, what would He see?

*70 days with Mark*

## If you don't ask...!

Although Jesus was a Jew, He came for people of all nationalities. He would listen to and help those who were prepared to believe in Him. In our story today the lady knew Jesus was the answer to her need. She recognised His power and authority and she humbly asked for His help.

**What did the woman ask Jesus to do for her? (v26)**

..................................................................

You may feel that you are not worthy of Jesus, like this lady felt, but she asked and received. Have you?

days with Mark

Wherever Jesus went, people flocked to hear Him, and when they heard how wonderful He was, they went and told others.

The man in our reading today couldn't do this. He couldn't hear the wonderful words of Jesus. Even if he could hear His words, he still could not tell others because he was dumb. This poor man was deaf and dumb. Jesus changed all this instantly when He met him. Now he could hear the wonderful Good News and tell others. Do you tell others the Good News about Jesus?

**?**

*How did the deaf and dumb man get to see Jesus? (v32)*

..................................................................

..................................................................

..................................................................

70 *days with* Mark

Mark 8:1–10

This story sounds very familiar. Didn't we read about it last week? No! That was another time when Jesus fed five thousand with five loaves and two fish.

**?** *How many loaves did Jesus use to feed the four thousand? (v5)*

.................................................................................

**?** *How many baskets of food were left over? (v8)*

.................................................................................

Jesus is so powerful and kind. He is always concerned for people's needs and is able to repeat many wonderful miracles.

## Proof and more proof

How slow those religious Pharisees were to believe Jesus. They had just seen Him feed over four thousand people with just seven loaves and a few fish. They still wanted more proof that He was from God.

**?** *Why were the Pharisees asking Jesus to do a miracle? (v11)*

..........................................................................................................

Jesus was not pleased with them. How much do you know about Jesus after reading these wonderful accounts of His life?

Do you believe, or do you feel you still need proof of who He is?

## Missing the point

How easy it is to be so concerned about everyday things like food and clothes. We soon forget about the more important things like learning about God. Today we read about how the disciples were misunderstanding what Jesus was saying to them.

***What do you think it means to have ears but not listen? (v18)***

They thought He was talking about bread, but He was talking about the wrong teaching of the religious leaders and how it could spoil their lives.

Mark 8:22–26

Jesus healed the man we read about, but at first he didn't see clearly (v24).

**?** *What did he see when he looked up? (v24)*

..................................................................

Jesus needed to touch him again (v25).

**?** *What did he see now? (v25)*

..................................................................

This time he saw things clearly, as they really are. This reminds us of the disciples who didn't seem to see things clearly. But, one day, they would see things as they really are. How is your understanding of Jesus? Do you see Him in the way that He wants you to see Him?

Peter was beginning to see and understand who Jesus really was (v29). 'You are the Christ,' Peter said. The 'Christ' was the 'Messiah' who all the Jews had been waiting for. They were looking for a Saviour who would save them from their sins and bring them back to a Holy God.

Jesus explains to His followers how He was going to die and then rise again after three days. Peter didn't like this and told Jesus not to go through with this. How did Peter think Jesus could be His Saviour? Again, Peter wasn't seeing clearly.

**?**

*Why do you think Peter reacted like this? (v32)*

...........................................

Mark 9:2–13

## The real thing

In the reading today, we see how some of Jesus' followers were growing in their understanding of Jesus.

 *Which disciples did Jesus take with Him up a high mountain? (v2)*

...........................................................................

For the first time they were to see Jesus as He really was. The God part of Him was shining through (v2, 3).

*What did God say from Heaven about Jesus? (v7)*

...........................................................................

What a wonderful experience this must have been for them. It reminds me of the blind man in Bethsaida who, at first, saw men like trees walking, but then saw clearly. Do you realise how very wonderful Jesus is?

## Super-power!

The source of all power comes from God. Jesus had the power to do all these wonderful miracles because He was God. Nothing was impossible with Jesus. How often do we put our hope and trust in other people and they let us down? Jesus will not let us down. The boy in our reading today was in a terrible state.

**?** *How long had the boy been sick? (v21)*

..........................................................................................

The disciples weren't able to help him, but Jesus was able, and what a difference He made to the boy's life.

**?** *What did the boy's father ask Jesus to give him more of? (v24)*

..........................................................................................

70 *days* *with* Mark

Mark 9:30–32

**?** *Who was Jesus talking to about His future? (v30–31)*

Sometimes we think we would like to know what is going to happen to us next week or next year. If something terrible was going to happen, I don't suppose we would like to know about it just now. Jesus knew about the future because He was and is God. Imagine what it must have been like for Jesus as He told His disciples about His death and resurrection. How He must have loved us, to know about all this, and continue to go through with it to be our Saviour.

**?** *What did Jesus' followers think about what He had told them? (v32)*

We all want to have JOY in our lives, don't we? Jesus teaches us the secret of obtaining real JOY.

J = Jesus first

O = Others second

Y = Yourself last

It is often hard to put this into practice in our own lives. The followers knew this too. In our reading today they were arguing about who was to be first or the greatest.

**? *Why do you think it is hard to put others before yourself?***

70 *days with* Mark

# The best judge

Here we read of the followers of Jesus trying to prevent others from doing miracles in the name of Jesus. I wonder if they were jealous and felt that they were the only ones that Jesus could use. Jesus certainly didn't prevent others. He knew their hearts and knew how sincere they were. We shouldn't judge others. Jesus is the only true judge.

**Who do you think is the only fair judge?**

# Children welcome

 **What did Jesus' followers say to the people who brought children to Jesus? (v13)**

........................................................

Have you ever heard the saying, 'Children should be seen and not heard'? Jesus would never have agreed with this. Children were very important to Jesus. Even when He was tired He still had time for them, and He never ignored them. You are very important to Jesus.

 **How did Jesus treat the young children? (v16)**

........................................................

**?** *What question did the rich young man ask Jesus when first meeting Him? (v17)*

..............................................................

We often think that if only we had more money, and were rich, we would be happy. This is very often not the case. This young rich man was sad (v22). His riches were more important to him than anything else, and yet they didn't bring him happiness. Knowing Jesus as our Saviour and putting Him first in our lives is the secret of true happiness.

**?** *Do we read that this rich man followed Jesus? (v22)*

..............................................................

Again, Jesus explains to His followers about what was soon to happen to Him.

**List some of the things that were going to happen to Jesus.**

....................................................................................

....................................................................................

....................................................................................

He knew every detail. How sad the followers must have been to hear this and yet they were amazed that Jesus should know these things. Slowly, they were beginning to understand how truly wonderful this man was. They had had the privilege of spending the last three years with Him. He certainly was more than a man.

## Me first!

Humility is a hard lesson to learn. We often want to be known and to be important so that others will think well of us. This is what James and John were like in our reading today.

**?** *What did James and John ask Jesus? (v37)*

..............................................................................

Jesus pointed out to them that they were not to be like this, if they were His followers. Jesus was the Creator of all things, the King of kings, and yet served others while here on earth.

**?** *What did Jesus come to do? (v45)*

..............................................................................

Are we following in the steps of Jesus?

70 days with Mark

Mark 10:46–52

*All important*

Have you ever felt small and unimportant? The man in our story today must have felt like this. He was blind and so was unable to work.

**?** ***How did the crowd treat this poor blind man? (v48)***

..............................................................

In those days these poor people were not helped by the government or caring organisations. They had to beg on the streets for money and food to survive. How sad this man must have been until he heard that Jesus was passing by. He knew that Jesus was the one man who could help him. He cried out to Jesus. Jesus heard his cry and healed him. Everyone is important to Jesus.

**?** ***How did the man show he was grateful to Jesus? (v52)***

..............................................................

Mark 11:1–14

When Jesus climbed onto the back of the untamed young donkey, He didn't have a problem riding it even though it had never been ridden before.

**?** *Why do you think Jesus was able to do this?*

..............................................................

The crowd of people who had gathered seemed to realise who Jesus was and so treated Him like a King. They sang praises to Him, but they only wanted Him to save them from the Romans who were ruling over them. They didn't realise that Jesus had come to save them from their sins.

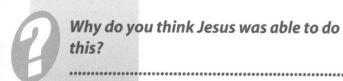

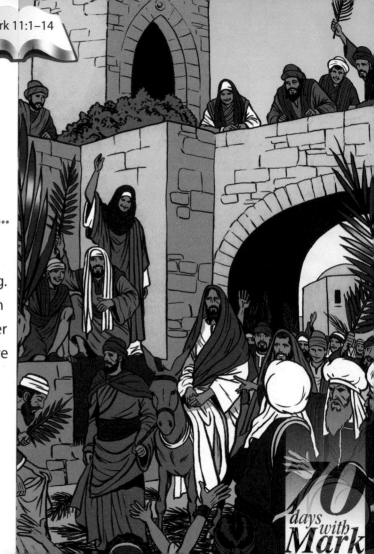

days with Mark

Mark 11:15–19

The temple was a building in Jerusalem where people could go and worship God and pray. Jesus was very sad and angry when He saw some people in the temple who had changed it into a place where they could make money for themselves unlawfully.

*What did Jesus do in the temple, to show that He was not pleased with their behaviour? (v15)*

How sad Jesus is when He sees things that are good spoilt by the sin of selfishness and greed.

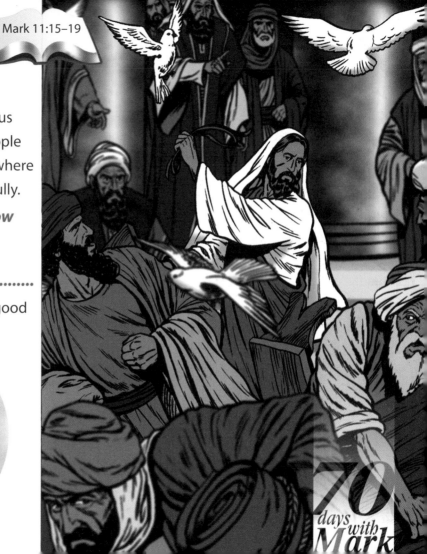

70 days with Mark

# It makes all the difference

**?** *What had happened to the fig tree? (v20)*

..............................................................................................

Jesus talks with His disciples about faith (trust), which can change situations and make a real difference. This faith must be in God alone, who is all-powerful and faithful. Have you ever trusted God in a difficult situation and seen God make a difference?

**?** *What did Jesus say we must do when we pray? (v25)*

..............................................................................................

# Mind reader

The religious leaders had seen Jesus perform many miracles. They still questioned Jesus about who He was, because they didn't believe He was from God. Jesus knew their minds and hearts and so He asked them some questions about John the Baptist. If they had answered the questions that Jesus had put to them, they would have shown what hypocrites they really were, so they remained silent.

**?** ***Who were the religious leaders afraid of? (v32)***

.....................................................................

Jesus knows all of our hearts and thoughts!

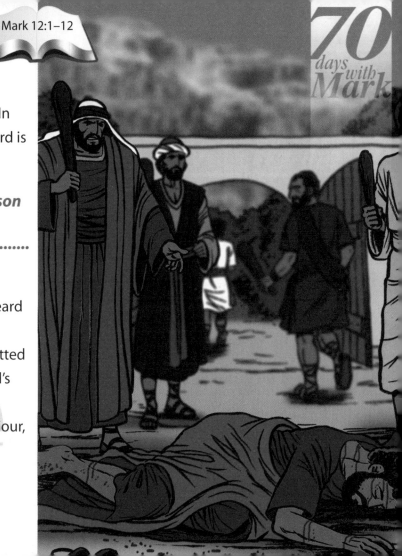

Everyone loves to hear a story. Jesus told many stories to teach important truths about Himself. In this sad story, the son of the owner of the vineyard is like Jesus.

**What did the wicked farmers do to the son of the owner of the vineyard? (v7–8)**

The farmers were like the Jewish leaders who rejected Jesus as God's Son. When the leaders heard this story, they knew exactly what Jesus was meaning. Their response was appalling. They plotted to kill Jesus. When you read and understand God's Word how do you respond to Jesus? Do you ask Him for forgiveness and receive Him as your Saviour, or do you reject Him as these Jews did?

Mark 12:13–17

How wise Jesus was. His enemies tried to trap Him so they could accuse Him of breaking the law. Jesus knew their hearts.

**What did Jesus ask the Pharisees to bring Him? (v15)**

........................................................................

**Whose picture was on the coin? (v16)**

........................................................................

No one can outsmart Jesus. Jesus points out that we should give God what belongs to Him. If you think about it, all things belong to God, as He is the Creator of all things, including us!

## Trick or treat?

The Sadducees were the next group of people to try and trick Jesus.

**?** *What didn't the Sadducees believe in? (v18)*

..........................................................................

In the end, it was they who ended up with a 'red face'. Jesus points out to them that they had been thinking wrongly because they didn't know the scriptures (the Bible). They were basing their ideas and beliefs on people's thoughts rather than on God's Word, the Bible. How important it is for us to get to know the Bible for ourselves so we can believe the truth.

70 days with Mark

Mark 12:28–40

## Questions, questions

Jesus was continually being questioned and He was never stuck for a wise answer. When asked about which of the commandments is the most important, He answered, 'To love God with every part of you', and secondly, 'To love your neighbour as you love yourself.' If you look at the commandments, the first four are all to do with our love for God and the last six are to do with our love for others.

 *Can you remember one of the Ten Commandments?*

...................................................................................

Mark 12:41–44

Jesus notices everything that is done for Him, however small it may seem. The poor widow did not know that she was being watched. She gave little (two small coins) compared to the rich people who gave large sums of money. The difference was that they still had much left while she had given all that she had. It's not how much we give to Jesus that pleases Him, but how much we have left!

*Why do you think the poor widow gave God all she had?*

*70 days with Mark*

The temple in Jerusalem was magnificent. It was greatly admired and thought to be indestructible. Jesus knew what the future held as He knows all things. About forty years later, the temple was destroyed by the Romans, just as Jesus had said it would be.

**How was Jesus able to know all these things?**

Mark 14:1–2

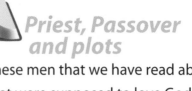

## Priest, Passover and plots

DAY 55

These men that we have read about were people that were supposed to love God. They were the leaders of the people, priests and teachers. In a few days' time, they would be celebrating the Passover, the Jewish feast. This is where they remembered God's goodness to their ancestors in saving them from death. Instead of preparing their hearts for this, they plotted to kill God's own Son.

*Why did they decide not to kill Jesus during the Passover feast? (v2)*

## All for Jesus

**What is the most precious thing that you own?**

...................................................................

Would you be willing to give it to Jesus? This lady was willing to give something very precious to Jesus.

**What did the woman do with her expensive gift? (v3)**

...................................................................

It was all because she realised who Jesus was and wanted to show Him. It cost her very much (v3). Jesus was pleased with her act of love. Other people criticised her. What do you think mattered most to the woman – the approval of Jesus or the people's disapproval?

**?** *Who was going to pay Judas to betray Jesus? (v11)*

........................................................

The love of money is such a temptation to some people it can cause them to do terrible things. It caused Judas to betray his best friend. He had been with Jesus for three years. He had seen His perfect life, His amazing miracles, and heard His wonderful words. His love of money was greater than his love for Jesus. Beware that the love of money isn't your downfall as you grow up!

**?** *Do you think Judas was happy about his decision, after he had received the money?*

........................................................

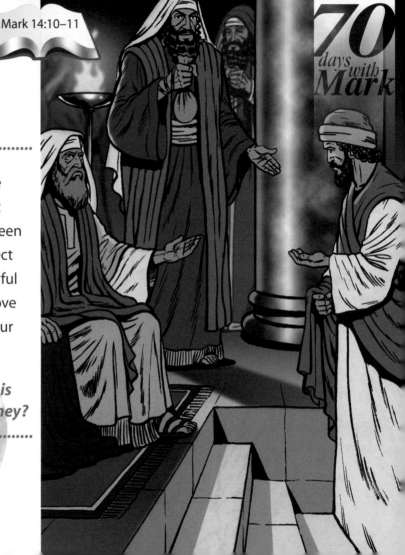

Mark 14:12–21

Jesus can never be taken by surprise. He knows all things. Jesus knew all about Judas and what he planned to do. Even so, He loved him and treated him just like the other disciples. Jesus gave Judas the opportunity to own up and change his mind. How gracious Jesus is!

*What would you do if you knew that someone who was supposed to be your friend was going to betray you?*

Once again, Jesus explains to His followers about His death that was soon to come. He used some simple visual aids to explain. The bread at the meal, which He was to break, was used to explain how His body would be broken. He used the wine as He poured it out to explain how that His blood would be poured out. How awful it must have been for Jesus to know about these things that were soon to happen to Him. He was willing to allow these things to happen to Him so that He could be the Saviour of the world!

**?** *Do you think Jesus could have prevented His death?*

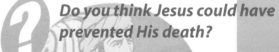

# Chicken!

How easy it is to say that we will be brave before an event, but when the event happens, we 'chicken out'! Peter was like this when he promised Jesus that he would be willing to die for Him. Jesus knew Peter, the future, and that Peter would deny that he knew Him.

**?** ***How many times did Jesus say that Peter would deny Him? (v30)***

...................................................................

Do you think that Jesus loved Peter any less for this? No! He knows all our failings before they even happen, but His love for us doesn't change!

70 days with Mark

# DAY 61 All alone

Mark 14:32–42

When we are worried or upset, it is good to have friends around us to support and help us. Jesus was facing a terrible time ahead and He knew that it was only a few hours away. He wanted His friends' support, but they fell asleep.

**?** *How many times did the disciples fall asleep? (v41)*

Jesus was all alone! Jesus knew all about the agony and suffering that He was to go through, and still He pressed on, knowing that this was the only way that we could have a Saviour.

Who were the large group of people that came to take Jesus away? Were they criminals and terrorists who were known for their evil? No! They were the priests, religious leaders, and one of Jesus' closest friends! (v43) There was another group of people who ran in the opposite direction. Who were they? Passers by? No! These were His closest friends, the disciples! (v50) How alone Jesus must have felt there in the garden.

**If you had been there, which group would you have been in?**

## Wasn't me!

 **Have you ever been blamed for something you didn't do? How did you react?**

.........................................................................

I expect you came out with a lot of words in your defence. When Jesus was accused, He was silent. The only time He spoke was when He was asked the question, 'Are you the Christ?' (the Deliverer). He answered, 'I am', which caused uproar. They believed that His answer to the question made Him guilty of death because they didn't believe that He was 'the Christ'.

**Why do you think the religious leaders found it so difficult to accept that Jesus was the Christ?**

.........................................................................

## A cockerel and a coward

The very thing that Jesus said would happen did happen. Peter said three times that he didn't know Jesus.

**?** *Are you ever ashamed to let people know that you follow Jesus, if you have believed on Him?*

................................................................

Peter was very sad when he realised what he had done. He remembered the promise that he had made earlier to Jesus. (Mark 14: 30)

**?** *Which is best – to be ashamed before God or before people?*

................................................................

70 days with Mark

Mark 15:1–5

Jesus was the Son of God, Creator of the entire world, and yet we read of how these men were so rough with Him (v1).

**?** *What did they do to Jesus? (v1)*

...........................................................

**?** *What had He done to deserve treatment like this?*

...........................................................

Not once do we read of Jesus 'getting His own back'!

*70 days with Mark*

Mark 15:6–20

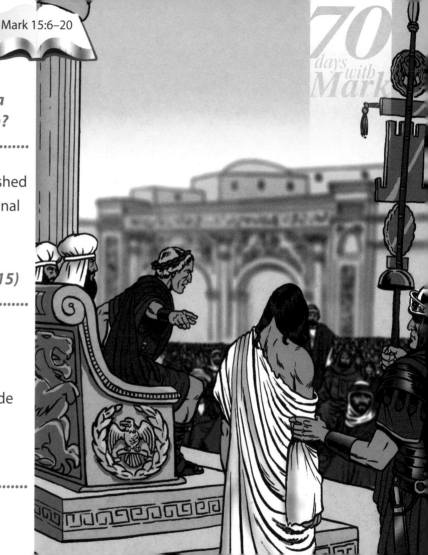

**If you had the choice, would you allow a bad man to be punished or a good man?**

..................................................................

The large crowd chose to allow Jesus to be punished for something He hadn't done, and chose a criminal to be set free! How strange!

**What was the name of this criminal? (v15)**

..................................................................

Stranger still, is when we realise that this same crowd, a few days earlier, had followed Jesus and shouted, 'Hosanna', and sang His praises as He rode on the donkey into Jerusalem.

**What choice would you have made?**

..................................................................

Mark 15:21–32

## The price is paid!

DAY 67

In this reading, we see just a little of the terrible suffering that Jesus went through on the cross: the pain as those nails were driven through His hands and feet; the mocking crowd; the other criminals; the taunting of the religious leaders.

They said, '…save yourself! Come down from that cross!' Jesus could have done this or He could have called ten thousand angels, but He willingly suffered, paying the price for all our sins.

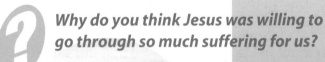

*Why do you think Jesus was willing to go through so much suffering for us?*

## Taking your place

The greatest suffering that Jesus went through was when God took the sins of the world and laid them on Jesus. In the three hours of darkness (v34), Jesus took the punishment for our sins. He was a substitute for you and me.

**? Why do you think God left Jesus alone? (v34)**

..................................................................

When Jesus cried in a loud voice (v37), it was a cry of victory. He had completed the work that He had been sent to do. Jesus died but, thankfully, that is not the end of the story!

**? Was Jesus paying for His own sins?**

..................................................................

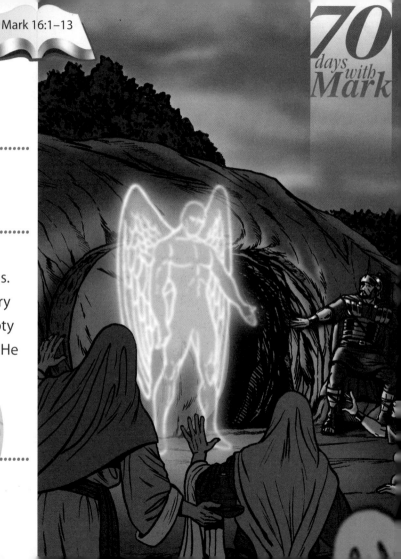

**DAY** **69** **Victory over death**

Mark 16:1–13

*70 days with Mark*

**?** *What were the women worried about concerning the tomb? (v3)*

..................................................................

**?** *Why did they not need to worry? (v4)*

..................................................................

Death is a terrible thing, but it couldn't hold Jesus. He was God. What a wonderful day it was for Mary and the other women when they found the empty grave. Jesus had risen from death just as He said He would!

**?** *How did the women react to what they saw? (v8)*

..................................................................

Mark 16:14–20

The disciples of Jesus shouldn't have been surprised at the resurrection of Jesus. He had told them many many times that it would happen. He tells them to go everywhere telling people the 'Good News'. Everybody needs to hear how Jesus has died for their sins and risen to life. They were now to carry on this work for Jesus. His work had been completed. When Jesus went back up to heaven, the followers did as Jesus had said. They went everywhere telling people the 'Good News'. Even today, His followers are doing the same.

**?** **Are you?**
.......................................................................

**?** *What is the Good News? (v15–16)*
.......................................................................

*70 days with Mark*

## International Children's Bible
### New Century Version

The International Children's Bible is different. It is not an adult Bible with a children's cover, nor is it an abridged version of adult text or a 'storybook' Bible. The ICB stands alone as the only totally new translation of the original Bible text – from the Greek and Hebrew language – specifically for children.

**Hardback:** 0-8500-9901-3          **Paperback:** 0-8500-9900-5

## International Children's Bible – New Testament
### New Century Version

This New Testament edition of the International Children's Bible includes delightful full-colour artwork and almost 100 black and white illustrations within the Bible text which makes the ICB text even easier to follow and understand for the 6–10-year-old reader. Also included: dictionary of Bible terms, colour maps, ICB family tree and translation notes.

**Hardback:** 1-86024-431-9          **Paperback:** 1-86024-432-7

## Amazing 3D Bible Story Books

These picture books bring Bible stories to life. Just pop on the attached glasses and see the amazing depth of the 3D illustrations, which will surely engage the minds of children and help them remember Bible stories.
**Each book contains one free 3D Viewer!**

Stories include *Jonah and the Big Fish, David and Goliath, Miracles of Jesus, and Parables of Jesus.*
**Miracles of Jesus:** 1-86024-504-8 **Parables of Jesus:** 1-86024-505-6 **David & Goliath:** 1-86024-507-2
**Jonah & the Big Fish:** 1-86024-506-4
Available from all Christian bookshops or visit our website at: **www.visual-impact-resources.co.uk**